Visible Mending for Beginners

© **Copyright 2019 - All rights reserved.**

The content contained within this book may not be reproduced, duplicated or transmitted without direct written permission from the author or the publisher.

Under no circumstances will any blame or legal responsibility be held against the publisher, or author, for any damages, reparation, or monetary loss due to the information contained within this book, either directly or indirectly.

Legal Notice:

This book is copyright protected. It is only for personal use. You cannot amend, distribute, sell, use, quote or paraphrase any part, or the content within this book, without the consent of the author or publisher.

Disclaimer Notice:

Please note the information contained within this document is for educational and entertainment purposes only. All effort has been executed to present accurate, up to date, reliable, complete information. No warranties of any kind are declared or implied. Readers acknowledge that the author is not engaging in the rendering of legal, financial, medical or professional advice. The content within this book has been derived from various sources. Please consult a licensed professional before attempting any techniques outlined in this book.

By reading this document, the reader agrees that under no circumstances is the author responsible for any losses, direct or indirect, that are incurred as a result of the use of information contained within this document, including, but not limited to, errors, omissions, or inaccuracies.

Table of Contents

Introduction _____ 8

Chapter 1: Stitches _____ 13

   Satin Stitch _____ 15

   Duplicate Stitch _____ 20

   Invisible Stitch _____ 22

   Cross Stitch _____ 31

   Eyelet Stitch _____ 36

   Rice Stitch _____ 39

Chapter 2: Historical Mending _____ 42

   Rafoogari _____ 42

   Sashiko Technique _____ 45

Chapter 3: How to Darn _____ 50

   Helpful Tips for Darning for Beginners __ 50

   Basic Darning _____ 54

   Mending the Holes in Your Favorite Sweater _____ 58

Darning a Sock _____ 61

5 Darning Tools _____ 65

Chapter 4: Patching Denim _____ 69

   Why should you NOT wash your jeans? _ 91

   How to mend and style thrift store finds _ 92

Chapter 5: 10 Sewing Tips! _____ 100

Conclusion _____ 106

References _____ 110

Introduction

Mending is the sewing of a cloth or clothing that is pierced or torn. Do you, too, have torn clothes that you would like to sew? If so, you will find what you are looking for in this book. While it is easy to find videos and visual guides on how to mend, there are not many written manuals about visible mending.

In this book, I will go over different mending methods and explain what you can do and how you can do it in detail. You will find lists of necessary equipment, steps to be followed to mend in different styles, and solutions to hide the mending. You will also learn about stitching distressed jeans, repairing socks, hemming jeans, and many more things.

The following chapters are all about versatile ways to mend different fabrics. It is true that a sewing machine is one of the most important investments in a seamstress's life. But when you are a beginner or you just want to learn how to stitch things by hand, a sewing machine is not necessary. This book will help you discover some alternatives to start slowly discovering the world of sewing before investing in a sewing machine.

The first thing you can do is start learning to sew by hand. Even if you own a sewing machine, sewing by hand remains relatively frequent since using a machine is not very practical when it comes to small things. Learning to sew by hand will be very useful for future projects and you can better understand how sewing works!

You will also learn about different, more traditional ways of stitching. A wrong choice of fabric can be disastrous when it comes to mending. This is a common mistake among beginners and can be hard to fix, but fortunately, it can be easily avoided with good preparation. With each section, you will have a list of things you need and tips and tricks that will help you achieve your best work.

When you sew by hand, you make stitches like those made by the sewing machine. There is a wide variety. These stitches are intended for particular purposes. For example, some serve to assemble two pieces of fabric, to finish a garment, or to make a specific piece. The chosen point also varies depending on the type of fabric with which you are working.

Sewing by hand seems simple. However, like any manual work, hand sewing requires a method. By following it, you have all the chances to succeed in what you undertake. I present you some general tips about sewing by hand and if you respect them, your work will be easier.

For sewing lovers who want to learn the basics, the following chapters are some techniques to learn basic ways to sew by hand. Through different projects, you will acquire more experience in sewing.

Chapter 1: Stitches

Before sewing, you must know how to thread a needle correctly. This may seem easy, since it is only a question of passing the thread in the eye of the needle. However, there are some precautions to take to avoid tangling the thread. Its length is very important. If it is too long, the thread may get tangled and you have to thread your needle again. Normally, you should cut a piece of thread about 50 cm long. If you do not have a measuring tape near you, this length is about the same as your arm, from shoulder to wrist. Once you have the right length, you cut the thread. Use a pair of scissors to cut, and don't rip/break the thread, because it will not slip through the needle well afterwards.

You hold the needle by putting the eye in front of a light to clearly distinguish the opening through which you pass the thread.

After the thread is through, you make a knot at

the end. If your vision is weak, you can use a needle threader. This is an instrument that makes it easier to pass the thread through the eye. First, you insert the opening of the needle threader into the eye of the needle. Then, you pass the thread through the opening of the needle threader and pull the threader back through the eye. This will thread your needle.

Before you start sewing stitches, you need to knot one end of the thread. Then, prick the needle into the fabric by pushing it from the back of the fabric toward the spot you want to stitch. To finish the stitching, make a knot in the shape of 8: make a small stitch, pass the thread inside the loop and pull. Do these two or three times to secure everything. The thread should not come undone if the knot is done correctly.

Things you will need:

- A needle, depending on the fabric you want to mend. For sewing, the needle must be fine if the fabric is fine. You will find the type of needle needed next to the fabric options to be mended below.

- Variety of threads (solid) depending on the type of the fabric. When you buy a spool of thread, it is generally indicated which fabric the thread is suitable for. If you have doubts, you can choose a thread suitable for all fabrics. In general, the color of the thread is chosen so that it is as close as possible to that of the fabric.

- A thimble, if you have one. The thimble is placed on the middle finger and is used to push the needle through the fabric, avoiding pain at the end of the finger.

- An embroidery hoop to help you stretch out the fabric.

Satin Stitch

A satin stitch is used a lot in embroidery and can

be used to cover imperfections. It looks like a solid, shimmery piece of fabric once it is completed. It is composed of very tight threads, in stitches of 3 to 13 cm in length. The stitches are close together, forming a solid image. When done correctly, the stitch will be illuminated by light and look absolutely stunning. Sewing a satin stitch by hand requires a certain level of precision. At first, practice on unused fabric. This way, you will have some experience, a good idea of the position of the points, and learn to sew them as tightly as possible without ruining your good fabric.

The Technique

- Use your embroidery hoop and tighten some fabric between the hoops. By doing this, the fabric will remain tense and flat during your work. Before you get into the complex patterns of satin stitch, start with trying to stitch a regular square or circle.

- Tie a knot at the end of your thread to stop it from escaping the fabric.

- Push the needle in from the bottom side of the fabric, where you want your shape to begin.

- Embed satin stitches as tightly as possible and do not exceed 1.25 cm in width. The satin stitches that are too long will float with space between the fabric and it will cause disorder.

- Tighten the points as much as possible. There must be no empty space between two points.

- Sew stitches as tight as possible without intermingling the threads, in parallel and narrow rows. Do this as slowly as possible to make sure you don't have to start over. Pay close attention to your work.

- Make sure the threads are evenly stretched with every new stitch.

Tips

Practice satin stitching until you get enough tight threads to lie flat, but loose enough not to deform the fabric. Sewing the points too tight is a classic mistake. Try to stretch the dots evenly or your threads will be too loose.

Make a satin stitch in your test fabric. Once you feel confident with your experience, move on to a real project.

Here are some ideas:

- Embroider the edge of a garment.
- Design the monogram of a project.
- Sew a buttonhole with a very narrow satin stitch.

When you feel ready, tackle a piece of art designed exclusively with satin stitches, and remember that all satin stitches must be tight.

The Best Fabrics for Satin Stitch

- **Aida fabric:** Commonly available in craft stores and absolutely perfect for beginners. It is 100% cotton and usually comes with a large variety of threads.

- **Fiddler's cloth:** A mix of polyester linen and cotton. It is very easy to stitch on and comes in different sizes.

- **Klostern:** A mix of rayon and cotton, easy to stitch on and fun to use.

- **Cotton:** A classic you can easily find anywhere. You are more likely to find items of cotton fabric around your home to practice your satin stitch.

- **Silk:** Can be hard to work with for a beginner but once you feel confident in your silk stitch, you will love working with silk fabric. It looks sophisticated and gorgeous with some silk stitching.

Duplicate Stitch

Duplicate stitch is also called Swiss darning. It allows you to go over your knitted project with stitches of a different color to add more dimension to it. When a duplicate stitch is done carefully, you should not be able to tell that the stitches are not knitted, without a close examination. This is a wonderful way of adding some color to your knitting projects without having the need to learn complicated knitting techniques.

The Technique

- Decide what shape you want, where you want to do your duplicate stitch, and how big you want it to be.

- Insert the needle on the bottom side, one line under where you want your design to start.

- It is better to start creating your desired stitch from the right side of the design.

- The trick is to follow the natural shape of the knitted fabric to make it look like your stitches are knitted- hence the name "duplicate stitch".

- Follow the line of the natural shape of the knit and find two legs you can push the needle through.

- When you push the needle through the two legs, you should have your first stitch that duplicates the fabric.

- Follow the natural shape of the knitted fabric back to the first spot you inserted your needle.

- When you complete two stitches, pass the needle through the back of the stitches vertically.

- Continue your desired shape by moving towards the left.

- Always remember to follow the shape of

the knit and finish by inserting the needle back where you started.

Here are some ideas:

- Make a flower on your knitted scarf.

- Add a heart on the outer side of your wool gloves.

- Duplicate stitch your initials on your beanie.

Remember!

Only use the same kind of thread you used for the knitted project while creating a duplicate stitch to make it look realistic.

Invisible Stitch

When sewing by hand, it is important to know the technique of the invisible stitch. This stitch will allow you to make liners or join two pieces of fabric without the thread being visible.

The sewing machine is our best friend in sewing, let's face it. But learning to sew by hand can sometimes also be very useful. In this section, you will learn how to sew an invisible stitch by hand. If you are a beginner and want to practice this stitch, you can sew your own washable cleaning wipes as a start.

If you are about to finish a cushion or other padded creation and you need to close it, nothing is simpler or more discreet than the invisible stitch.

Necessary tools for this stitch:

- A thimble

The Technique
- Get a thin needle.

- Take the needle and pass some sewing thread of the same color as your fabric through the needle eye.

- Choose a thread of the same color as your

fabric. Even though this stitch is, as its name indicates, "invisible," it is better to be smart and to remain uniform.

- Iron the two edges to be connected by marking a clean fold. With this trick, the work will be easier and smoother.

- Immobilize the fabrics you want to sew with some pins. Keep the pins close to the area you want to stitch but not directly on the area.

- Make your first stitch by passing the needle under one of the fabrics, where the fold is. This will hide the knot.

- Then go to the opposite side and slide the needle through the second fabric horizontally.

- Go back to the first fabric and slide the needle horizontally to pick up the fabric.

- Go back and forth on one side and then

the other.

- Use the straight stitch technique and do not hesitate to hold the two edges firmly between your fingers, thus avoiding irregular points.

- Pull the thread as you go along to shut the fabrics together.

- From your first stitch, your goal is to make long stitches on one side of the piece of fabric and short stitches on the other side.

- You must now be very careful when entering and removing the needle from the fabric to create the seam to make the thread invisible or almost invisible.

- When you get to the end, pick up some more fabric from inside the fold like before and create a thread loop. Push your needle through the loop twice to secure the thread.

- To hide the thread, pierce the needle through the fold and bring it out from inside the fabric. Bunch up the fabric to shorten the thread and cut the thread. This will hide the end of your thread perfectly.

The Technique for Sewing a Pillowcase

A pillowcase has four sides, and if you want to put the stuffing into the case, you'll need to use an invisible stitch to close one of the four sides of the pillowcase. To start, choose your two pieces of fabric that will make the font and the back of the pillow case. Place the fabric on top of each other, with both "outside" sides facing each other. You want the sides that will be on the outside of the pillow to be facing each other and away from you while you sew them together. Pin the fabric pieces together so they don't move. Start by using a regular straight stitch or back-stitch to go around the three sides of the pillowcase, sewing them together. You could also do those three sides with a sewing machine. You should use a thread that matches the color of the pillowcase. Once you have three sides sewn, flip the fabric through the open end of the pillowcase so that the inside pieces are now facing each other, and the outside pieces are facing you. Put your stuffing, or inner pillow inside the pillowcase. Now it's time to use the invisible stitch for the last side of the pillowcase to close everything up. Follow these steps for the invisible stitch:

- Choose a thread of the same color as your fabric. Even though this stitch is, as its name indicates, "invisible," it is better to be smart and to remain uniform.
- Taking the fourth, unclosed side of the pillowcase, fold the two edges inside the pillow case. Then iron the crease to make

a clean fold. You are going to use the crease of the fold to sew, so it's important that it is a sharp crease.

- To make your first stitch, thread the needle, tie the knot at the end of the thread, place the needle inside the pillow, and pass it through one of the creases on the edge. This will hide the knot of the thread and leave the needle outside of the pillowcase with the thread attached.
- Then, take the needle over to the other fold. Slide the needle through the crease, following the crease line. You're just skimming the needle under the fabric and back up on the same crease. It should be similar to a running stitch.
- Once the needle appears again, pull the thread through, and then bring the needle back to the other crease. Follow the same pattern; slide the needle through the crease following the crease

line.
- Continue this pattern back and forth, going over the open gap of the pillowcase and making all of your stitches in the crease of the folds. Your thread across the gap should look like the rungs of a ladder.
- Try to make all of your stitches an even length.
- When you pull the thread to close the gap, your stitches will shut the two pieces of fabric together and you shouldn't be able to see the stitches at all.
- Keep going until you reach the end of the gap and pull the thread to close the gap. Your fourth side should now be closed, and any stuffing should not be exposed.
- When you get to the end, pick up some more fabric from inside the fold like before and create a thread loop. Push your needle through the loop twice to secure the thread.

- To hide the thread, pierce the needle through the fold and bring it out from inside the fabric. Bunch up the fabric to shorten the thread and cut the thread. This will hide the end of your thread perfectly.

Tips:

- This technique is also called the mattress point or the hidden point.

- Use the thread of the color of the piece of fabric that will be most exposed to sight. This way, your seam will be much less visible.

- If you use thin, long needles, your aim will be better, and the holes will be smaller.

- Pay attention to your fingers and take the necessary precautions when sewing like using a thimble.

Here are some ideas:

- Use this technique when hemming pants, skirts or other clothing items.
- Use it to finish blankets or pillowcases.
- Use it whenever you desire a perfect finish where the thread won't be visible.

Cross Stitch

Very different from traditional embroidery techniques, and much easier, the technique of cross-stitch embroidery is performed by a succession of small crosses that are embroidered on top of each other to form a pattern. Often, you will hear "counted stitches" instead of cross stitch. Indeed, to achieve embroidery, it is necessary to count the number of small crosses to form the pattern. You know how to count, so you'll know how to embroider!

Necessary tools:

- Embroidery cloth

- A needle

- Embroidery thread

- A pair of embroidery scissors

- A cross stitch pattern (printed out, cut out, etc.)

There is a canvas made especially for cross stitch embroidery. Beginners always start by embroidering on an Aida canvas. It is ideal to begin with because it is woven with small holes that show the place where you will insert your needle.

The Technique
- Tie a knot at the end of the thread and take your needle from the bottom side of the fabric, on the same line as the start of your embroidery.

- Bring the needle to the front of the canvas on the starting point of your first cross-stitch.

- Start embroidering through the knot, making sure to cross over the thread on the back with each stitch to secure it.

- Hold the tail of the thread against the back of the fabric in the direction that you will embroider and work the first 4 to 5 points on this thread each time.

- Make sure the dots cover the thread on the back of the fabric and cut the end of the thread to continue embroidering.

- Once your project has begun, you can secure the new stitches by passing them under several points adjacent to the back and continue embroidering.

Tips

- Start embroidering the model from the

center of the canvas and go from corner to corner. For beginners and all other embroiderers, it is best to start in the middle and avoid a miscalculation.

- When embroidering, make sure your stitches are flat. If your thread begins to spiral, let go of the needle and let it hang. The thread unravels itself.

- Make sure your points all cross in the same direction.

- Keep your tension and your points equal while embroidering your model.

- First, work the areas with markings and then fill the bottom.

- Work dark colors and then light colors.

- Sometimes you will embroider a few stitches for one area and then you will embroider in another area with the same color of thread. Moving from one area to another with the same thread may seem easier than stopping and picking up another thread, but if you keep the same color, the thread can be seen on the back of the canvas and make it visible at the location.

- Keep the same thread uncut only if the gap is small between the two areas and the thread is a light color.

- When you want to tie beads with cross-stitch, first work the cross-stitch diagonal, then tie the beads when you work the back row. Make sure you use good quality beads because the plastic beads melt under the iron.

Here are some ideas:

- Put on crystal beads, crystals, charms, and small buttons. These can be interesting creative touches on a cross stitch pattern. 3D ornaments add interest to any embroidery and are available in many colors and styles.

Eyelet Stitch

Also known as the "star stitch", this stitch belongs to the counted stitches family. This is a very decorative stitch that can be used especially in traditional embroidery.

It usually consists of 8 branches in front that all meet in the center. The center then looks like an eye.

Eyelet is a simple stitch that you find a lot in embroidery, but if it is poorly done it lacks beauty. It is embroidered from the outside towards the center and you pull your thread to make a hole in the center.

Necessary Tools:

- Punch Awl

The Technique

- Draw a circle on your fabric.

- Punch the fabric with the awl until the edges of your circle meet the tool.

- The hole will be the center of your eyelet stitch.

- Stitch a circle around the center using the straight stitch technique. Start as far or as close to the fabric as you want, depending on the size you want your eyelet stitch to be. Your stitched circle does not need to be perfect as it will be hidden by the branches of the eyelet stitch later.

- When you are done with your circle, pull the needle out from the center hole.

- Pick a stitch out of the circle and start creating your first branch by taking the needle back down in the hole and piercing the fabric right on the circle stitch you picked from the bottom.

- We are using the circle you stitched as a guideline.

- When you piece the fabric from the bottom, don't pull it all the way out.

- While your needle is still in the fabric, take the thread and bring it behind the needle to the opposite side.

- Pull your needle out.

- You should have your first branch now.

- Push the needle through the hole and pierce the fabric right next to your first branch.

- Bring the thread behind the needle and pull your needle out to create your second branch.

- Continue doing this until your circle is

covered in branches and you can no longer see the stitched circle.

- To finish it off, flip the fabric to the wrong side, and pick the thread of a couple of the branches without the needle going through the fabric.

- Create a loop and bring your needle and thread through the loop to secure the stitch.

Rice Stitch

This stitch is obtained by alternately knitting a stitch and a reverse stitch on the same row, then thwarting the stitches on the next row. The number of stitches must be a multiple of 2.

It can sometimes be scary, but it will become very easy if we stay focused on the work and the finished product is very beautiful.

The Technique

- This technique is best done on knitted fabric.

- Start by putting the needle through the bottom of the spot you want your design to start from.

- It is very important to note that the rice stitch is always worked on a base of even stitches. If you have an odd number of stitches, the stitch will not come outright. This is how a small mistake in your knitting can sometimes distort the whole project.

- Make your first stitch up towards the right side to start.

- Bring the thread back to the starting point of the work so you can do the next stitch upside down.

- Do the next stitch upside down, like an

"X", then bring the thread back by passing it between the two legs to knit the next stitch.

- Continue by alternating row 1 and row 2 along the length desired to make your stitch knit.

Here are some ideas:

- Rice stitch works like cross-stitch but on knitted fabrics.

- Try using this technique instead of the duplicate stitch when you want a more detailed design on your knitted project.

Chapter 2: Historical Mending

Rafoogari

Rafoogari is an old, dying Indian technique of stitching. It is the ability to repair precious materials such as silk and cashmere. Rafoogari is an old art form, in which holes are stuffed so artfully that the points at which the fabrics were mended together should not be noticeable.

The Technique

- Working with your extra fabric, cut a piece that covers the hole in your garment. Make sure the piece is larger than the hole by at least 1 cm on each side.

- Pin the piece to your fabric inside the garment, so that the edges of the piece are not seen on the outside of the garment. When you have the garment facing you, with the outside fabric facing you, you should be able to see the hole, but also see your extra fabric inside the hole. Now it's time to stitch.

- Check the garment's stitching pattern. Is it a very fine stitch, or are they wider stitches with more gaps in them? You will need to follow the same stitching pattern in the same stitching direction.

- Using that pattern, sew along the edges of the piece you've placed over the hole. Then sew over the hole and the extra fabric using a running stitch and following the direction and size of the stitches of the garment. When you are finished, the hole should be completely hidden and seem to disappear into the fabric.

- You can do this with a sewing machine so that it goes quicker, or you can do it by hand in a more traditional way. Either way, go slowly, check your fabric often, and make sure your stitches are not standing out too much.

While it is a beautiful form of art on its own, people don't want to mention that they are wearing old pieces of fabric mended together. In cultures like the Indian culture, it might even be considered shameful; therefore, people no longer use this mending technique as much as they used to. Because of how hard it is to master, the low demand, and how much work it requires, Rafoogari has been slowly disappearing. In modern times, textile artists highlight the holes or space between the fabrics with colorful threads and plant fibers to try to bring the dying art form back to life. Working constructively with weaknesses creates a new way of performing this technique.

Sashiko Technique

When translated from Japanese, sashiko means "small seams". The sashiko technique is sewn on the front of the fabric with visible stitches that are the size of a grain of rice. It uses a thick white thread on an indigo fabric made of vegetable fibers (flax, hemp, glycine). Cotton usage appeared more recently, and its use has become more common at the end of the 19th century.

Recently, Sashiko has become a very decorative embroidery technique used throughout the house: curtains, bags, clothes, tablecloths, etc. It's also used to strengthen the clothes of judo, kendo.

Followers of the traditional sashiko will do it on a more or less thick cotton cloth (kimono cloth) with a specific white thread. But it can be made on any fabric you choose, including cotton, linen, silk, wool, or on one with more thicknesses.

The Technique

- Specific cotton yarns are used in 1 or more strands but also pearl cotton, embroidery cotton, silk thread, mixed thread, metal, etc. can be used.

- Stitch on the front of the fabric, about 5 to 8 stitches per inch (= 2.5 cm). For example, quilting 8 to 12 stitches per inch, made without counting the frame or the border of the fabric.

- Needle, stitch length, and thread thickness needs to be adapted to the work according to thickness and type of work you are looking for.

To patch a hole or rip in your jeans, you can use the Sashiko technique to make it decorative. You will need spare fabric, the garment that needs to be repaired, and thread of a different color from your garment. The thread has to be a different color because it's not meant to blend in. Sashiko should stand out.

- First, find a fabric to use as a backing for the hole. It can be colorful, or the same color as the garment you're repairing.
- Pin the fabric to the jeans on the inside of the jeans leg. Remember to be careful while pinning and sewing. You don't want to accidentally sew your jeans closed. So, make sure that your pins are only connecting your spare fabric to the side of the jeans you want to sew.
- Choose a pattern you would like to sew onto the jeans. A really simple pattern is to use a wide-spacing running stitch in one direction, or both directions. You can also choose a pattern like a cross, boxes, waves, etc.
- Once you have your pattern, it's time to sew. Using your different colored thread, sew your pattern, starting from above

your patch and continuing to below your patch. Once you are finished, tie off your thread and cut it.

Now you have a pair of beautifully decorated and patched jeans. This method can be used on a variety of fabrics and for a variety of reasons. It's mostly decorative, but it can easily be used for mending.

Most often, today, sashiko is made on a single layer of fabric. It can also sometimes be associated with patchwork.

It can be done on two or more layers by adapting the length of the stitches according to the thickness of the work:

2 layers of fabric (the 2nd being the lining)

1 layer of fabric + 1 layer of fleece: choose a fleece with little bulk: cotton or polyester, old towels or wool can do the trick! Beware of polyester fleeces whose fibers may come out

with the embroidery (choose a dark colored fleece if the top fabric is dark). The lining is added later.

1 thickness of fabric + 1 thickness of fleece or other + 1 thickness of fabric (lining)

In principle, sashiko is not a reversible embroidery technique. So, you must be careful when attempting it. The changes of direction will be concealed in the thickness of the work if you can hide it well. Sometimes, the threads are grouped and knotted in the corners of the garment to give it a smoother appearance.

Chapter 3: How to Darn

The times have changed, but it remains useful to know how to handle thread and needle. Here is a complete guide to the repair of clothing help you fix everything you need from sweaters and socks to jeans and pillows.

Helpful Tips for Darning for Beginners

The sewing box

- No need for a huge sewing box: the basic materials will fit in a shoebox or in a cookie tin perfectly.

- Pin the sewing and darning needles of different sizes into a pincushion or a piece of soap (the soap will help them slip more easily into thick, stiff fabrics). A magnet can also serve as a pincushion and will allow you to quickly pick up scattered needles.

- The pins and safety pins can be stored in a small box of matches.

- In addition, you will need sewing and darning thread in various colors, and possibly solid thread for thicker fabrics.

- Complete your box with a thimble, a darning ball, a quick-pick and scissors. A needle threader will also be useful.

- Over time, many buttons will accumulate in your box. To see more clearly, put together those that have the same color. As for the spare buttons, keep them in transparent bags, with a label indicating the name of the corresponding garment.

Buttons and boutonnieres

- Buttons can come loose or fall; it happens. Before losing it, at the risk of not finding a substitute, it is better to take the time to sew it securely.

- To avoid damaging the fabric by disassembling the button, slide a comb between the fabric and the button. Then remove the remnants of the thread;

- Rub the thread with candle wax to stabilize it;

- Sew the four-hole button stitch, preferably crosswise with two threads. So, if one of them breaks, the button stays in place;

- To prevent the fabric of the button band from tearing, especially on the coats, sew another small button on the wrong side.

- Close a buttonhole that is distended or too big by stitching it upside down: make a few points from the outside to the center, so that the button just goes through. Stop the end with the thread.

Quick troubleshooting

- For stretch fabrics, sew the edges of the piece by hand.

- Holes in the wool should be hemmed, to prevent them from getting larger.

- To repair torn jeans, take a piece of other jeans that you no longer wear and sew it on the hole, inside.

- To easily thread a needle, spray some hairspray on the end of the thread.

- Transparent nail polish or the glue can certainly stop a mesh that pulls, like pantyhose, but remember that it cannot be repaired. It is therefore better to reserve this solution for emergencies. If you are not home when the problem occurs, apply moistened soap.

- Rub zippers with beeswax if they are

hard to open and close. As for reused zippers, spray them with starch water, and then iron them: you can then sew them onto another garment.

- Replacing an elastic is a breeze: attach the new elastic to the old one with a safety pin. Then remove the old one by gently pulling it: the new one will be put in place by itself.

- Threads will be stronger if you coat them with paraffin wax or wax.

- Do you have no thread of the right color on hand? Choose a darker tone than the original. Do not use a lighter thread.

Basic Darning

- Before you start sewing stitches, you need to knot one end of the thread. Then, prick the needle into the fabric by pushing it from the back of the fabric toward the spot you want to darn.

- You have to sew from right to left and leave a small regular space between each point. Take the needle out of A, replant it in B and take it out in C, and so on. With practice, you will learn to do 2-3 stitches without taking the needle out of the fabric.

- Finish the seam with one or two back stitches.

- To finish the stitching, make a knot in the shape of an 8: make a small stitch, pass the thread inside the loop and pull. Do this 2 or 3 times to secure everything.

Darn a Hemline

- Fold the fabric after determining the width of the hem;

- Iron it, then secure it with pins;

- Sew the inside edge with the slipper

stitch, from left to right, so that the hem does not get loose.

- Avoid stretching the thread too much.

- Then, iron the hem with a damp cloth between the iron and the fabric.

Pattern Darning

Things you will need:

- A very thick cardboard

- A long-blade cutter or a mini-saw or a sharp knife with teeth

- Wide elastic bands

The Technique

- Cut a hole in the center of your cardboard.

- Put your garment around the cardboard and stabilize it with the elastics.

- Start about 1 cm from the edge of the

hole, making a stitch line in regular stitches.

- Keep going up until about 1 cm from the other side of the hole.

- When you reach the other side, go towards the direction of the hole and do the same thing.

- Continue until a square of stitches is formed around the hole.

- Stitch your way into the hole by continuing to stitch smaller squares.

- When your hole is covered loosely with the first stitch square, start stitching another square on top of the one you just stitched but create a pattern by going in the opposite direction so that the stitches create an "X".

- If your fabric is fragile or thin, do not pull too much on your thread; you will create the risk of tearing the fabric in another spot.

Mending the Holes in Your Favorite Sweater

There are multiple ways you can fix a hole in your sweater. If it is very small, just stitch it with some thread and needle by holding the fabric together. If the hole is as big as the width of your finger or bigger, use one of the techniques below.

Technique 1

Things you will need:

- Thread to match your sweater's thread
- A needle
- A darning mushroom, hard-boiled egg (cold), or lightbulb.
- Washable sewing marker, or disappearing ink sewing marker.

The Technique

- With the right side of the sweater facing you, place a darning mushroom, egg, or a lightbulb inside the sweater and under the hole. This will stabilize the hole for your sewing.

- Start by stitching around the hole to help prevent it from getting any larger. Place the stitches about ¼ inch away from the edge of the hole and use a running stitch or back stitch to go around the hole until you return to the starting point. Tie off the thread.

- To mend the hole, draw a square over it with the sewing marker. The square should be larger than the hole, with at least 1 cm of space above, below, and to the sides of the hole.

- Using a running stitch, fill in the square vertically. Make sure the stitched columns are close together and alternate the stitches. When you get to the hole, pass the thread over it and continue the running stitch past the hole.

- When you've completed the square with running stitches, go over it again, but this time horizontally. Weave the threads into the running stitch you made, moving back and forth. When you get to the hole, weave the thread between the stitches you made that passed over the hole. It should look like a basket weave when you are finished. Tie off the thread, pass the knot into the inside of the sweater, and cut the thread.

Technique 2

Things you will need:

- A couple of pieces of paper
- Scissors
- Fusible fabric
- An iron

The Technique

- Draw the desired shapes on the paper.

- Cut out the shapes.

- Turn the shapes over and place them on the lapel of the fabric (fusible side).

- Draw the outline with a pen.

- Cut out the fusible fabrics.

- Place the fusible parts on the area to be repaired and fix them on the iron (maximum temperature and pressure).

Darning a Sock

Few people today really know how to darn socks even though it is not that complicated. Instead of throwing your socks out, you can choose to darn them and keep using them. So, what to do when one of your socks is punctured?

The Technique

- Choose the right thread! Choose a thread. You must choose one whose color and thickness are as close as possible to those of your perforated sock.

You can also choose a dark thread for horizontal seams and a lighter color for vertical seams. If you have a sock of dark color, you can use white thread to see more clearly when you stitch and vice versa.

The thread you choose does not have to be the same color as the sock (unless you're a foot model, not many people will look at the seams of your socks).

- Thread the thread into the needle. Do it twice if the sock is thicker.

- Tie a knot at the end of the thread to fit the needle. Then start sewing the inside of the sock, so that the knot is not seen from the outside.

- Put a darning egg in the sock.

- If you do not have a darning egg or do not want to buy one, you can use a small round object instead, such as a tennis ball or a light bulb. You can also use your hand and slip it into the sock, as if it were a foot. However, this last option will make the task more difficult.

- Stitch the hole shut.

When the sock has thinned out

- Take the sock.

- Cut out the little threads that protrude from your sock. Using scissors, cut the sock so that the hole is more visible and easier to sew. Be careful not to enlarge the hole as well.

- Push the needle at one end of the hole. Then pass it on the other side of the hole, so that both ends are glued together. This is called a straight stitch, which is the most basic of the stitches.

- All you have to do is put your needle through the hole several times, so that the ends of the hole are connected to each other by the thread.

- You can also make a few stitches above the hole to reinforce the seam so that the hole does not reappear later.

- Repeat this operation. Continue until the hole is completely sewn and covered with thread.

- You can now make points perpendicular to those you have just done (optional). This will further enhance the stitching you just created. For this, simply move your needle over the parallel points.

Tips!

- Try to stitch your sock before the hole is

too big. Remember the adage: "prevention is better than cure"! If you darn your sock quickly, it will take less time and effort than if you wait too long.

- Be careful not to hurt yourself with the needle by threading or sewing. Wear a thimble if you are afraid of hurting yourself.

5 Darning Tools

Darning Egg

A darning egg. The haberdashery egg is made of wood but, failing that, one can take a chicken egg, hard-boiled preferably to avoid accidents.

How to use it?

- The principle is to replace the worn part by weaving crossed threads.

- Place the egg in the sock under the darning area and hold the egg and sock together in your left hand.

- Thread 1 to 4 strands of darning wool together in the needle (4 if it is a big hole in a big sock, 1 only if you just have to reinforce a beginning of wear). Do not tie knots.

- Begin 0.5 cm in width and height of the worn part.

- Make a row of straight stitches from 1 to 2 mm thick, from right to left.

- Turn the work half a turn to make a second row of staggered dots, 1 to 2 mm from the first.

Darning Mushroom

The darling mushroom is a first cousin of the darning egg. It belongs to the big family of sewing objects. It is usually composed of a half ball flattened and a handle, which, for the mushroom, serves as a foot!

It has the same use as his cousins: put it in the

damaged garment and place it at the level of the hole, in order to mend it. The cap of the mushroom makes it possible to maintain the tensioned fabric in order to facilitate the recovery or the staking of the perforated part. It offers a larger area for a wider recovery.

The wood used is very often a hardwood like oak or boxwood, which takes a nice texture over time. Some are left natural, and some are painted. They come in various sizes.

Tape measure

The tape measure is a must when talking about sewing equipment. It allows you to take measurements easily and accurately. Whether it is to take your measurements, check the width of fabric, or measure the length of fabric you need for your project, it is simply essential.

Marker pen

They are soluble with water. They are used to mark the fabric before making cuts or stitches to create the perfect end result.

Tailor's scissors

These are big scissors (at least 20 cm long) intended to cut fabric and nothing but fabric!

The tailor's scissors are valuable and become dull if they are not used wisely. So, hide them, put a padlock on them, and threaten whoever approaches them. If they are used on anything other than fabric, they will be ruined.

Chapter 4: Patching Denim

Raw denim (without spandex) is a very stiff material especially if you are a follower of the skinny jean trend. Friction caused by walking tends to have an abrasive effect especially if your jeans are too wide or too big. You will quickly have holes in the hems, ankles, and buttocks, especially if you walk a lot in your day to go to work for example. On the other hand, if it is too small, the seams will have the annoying habit of letting go and ripping, especially around the thighs.

In short, if you want to keep your jeans for a long time, beyond choosing quality materials, you must be careful to take it to the right size with a cut adapted to your body type. The adjustment of the hems is also important because it allows you to stretch your legs and avoid the multiple folds that will rub against each other. This is all because fixing a hole in your jeans is not as easy as just stitching them back up. They will not look exactly the same as before.

Thankfully, there are techniques you can follow that will allow you to fix the hole in your denim clothes without cutting them into shorts. Let's look at a couple of the solutions below.

Fixing the Crotch

The crotch of a jean undergoes all kinds of wear: it is stretched, rubs against the thighs, and the seam can rip at the worst possible time. The crotch is the part that is most likely to crack or tear and create large or small holes. Instead of giving up and tossing damaged jeans, you can use various methods to repair them. A small tear can be sewn while for a larger hole, you will need a piece of cloth.

- Cut the threads that hang around the damaged part. You can repair small holes without extra fabric, simply by sewing the edges of the hole or torn part together. Before doing so, take scissors and cut the strings protruding from the edges of the hole so that they are clear. Otherwise, the strings will hinder you when you sew. When cutting the strings, be careful not to enlarge the hole.

- Cut only the threads that protrude, not the fabric itself.

- Thread a needle and knot the thread correctly. If you tie the opposite end of the thread, it will remain anchored in the fabric when you start sewing. It can be annoying to have to thread the needle constantly, so be sure to catch the thread.

- Sew the edges of the hole to prevent them from fraying even more. Reinforce the edges of the damaged part by "closing" them with small looping dots. Be careful not to make these dots so close to the edges that the thread simply damages more of the jean's fabric. This step is optional, but it can help prevent the fabric around the hole from fraying and make your repair more resistant.

- The scallop and buttonhole stitch are good choices for this step.

- Sew the hole in the garment to close it. Flatten the fabric or hold it so that the hole in the jeans is completely closed. Make a vertical seam over the hole to close it. You may need to iron several times for the repair to be resistant. Begin the dots about 1 cm from one of the edges of the hole. Finish them about 1 cm from the other edge of the hole.

- As you pass the other side of the hole, make points smaller and smaller.

- Pull the thread to tighten it, knot it and cut off the end so that nothing sticks out

- These points should be at least 1 cm away from those you have sewn to reinforce the edges of the hole.

- You can also do this at the sewing machine, but if the hole is very small, it can be just as easy to repair by hand.

Adding Fabric to the Crotch

- Cut the thread protruding around the hole. Using a piece of fabric is ideal if you do not feel like you are able to sew or simply want to do a quick repair. This might be a good solution for a work jean whose utility is more important than appearance.

- Cut out a piece of fabric the right size. Flip the jeans over and take a piece of fabric over old jeans or use any other piece of fabric that you want to sew on the hole. Make sure there is plenty of fabric well around the torn part so that you can apply glue.

- Put some textile glue on the piece. Follow the specific instructions on the bottle. In general, apply the glue to the edges of the fabric. Be careful not to put glue on the part of the fabric that will be seen on the outside of the jeans. Place the fabric on the hole, press it down and hold it in place.

- The drying time depends on the glue used, but it should not be longer than a few hours.

Use a fusible fabric

- Prepare the hole to repair. A fusible fabric is a simple solution if you do not want to sew it on. As with all other methods, first cut the threads so that the edges of the fabric are clean then turn the jeans and prepare the fabric that you will stick with the iron. Measure the hole with a measuring tape and cut the fabric to the correct size, making sure it is at least 1 cm wider around the hole.

- You can measure the fabric by eye, but with a tape measure, you are less likely to deceive yourself and waste the product by cutting a piece too small.

- If you cut rounded corners, the fabric will be less likely to come off.

- Place the fabric on the outside of the hole. If you stick it on the wrong side, the two sides of the pants could merge. If this happens, the leg of your jeans might remain closed and you won't be able to put your legs through.

- Iron the fabric on. Once your iron is hot, put the fabric on the hole and iron it. The time you must keep the iron on the fabric depends on each type of fusible fabric, so read the instructions and stick to them.

In general, do not leave the iron in place for more than thirty to sixty seconds.

- Once the fabric glue is dry, your jeans will be ready.

Sewing a Piece of Fabric to Repair a Larger Hole

- Find a piece of suitable fabric. Sewing a piece of fabric is the most effective way to repair a big hole in the crotch, but also the one that requires the most work. You must have basic skills in hand sewing, but when you're done, the result should be cleaner and more resistant than a bonded or heat-sealed fabric. Start by finding a piece that fits the hole in your jeans.

- If you put the fabric on the back of the pants, choose a color as close as possible to that of your jeans so that the repair is not seen too much.

- If you want to have fun or do something light, you can let your creativity run wild when you choose the fabric.

- Make sure the fabric is not thicker than your jeans. If it is not flexible enough to follow your movements, the fabric will tear.

- Cut out a piece of fabric that is at least 2.5 cm larger than the hole. If you cut the fabric parallel to the warp or weft, the edges are more likely to fray.

- Lay the jeans flat and pin the fabric on it. Make sure the fabric is not wrinkled or taut; otherwise the extra fabric will be taut or will form a lump. Unless you want to patch the damaged part with colorful or very showy fabric, slip the fabric inside the jeans to keep it in place.

Hemming Jeans

It's almost impossible to find jeans at the right

leg length when you buy them in stores. If you have found a pair that suits you but is too long, you can bring it to a tailor or make a hem yourself. You can keep the original hem, or you can make a new one. Remember that it can be difficult to work with jeans, but by following a few simple methods, you can ensure a successful result.

Keep the original hem

- Decide on the location of the hem. Try the jeans and decide where you want to put the hem. In general, jeans should be between 2 and 3 cm above the ground. This will prevent you from stumbling and having pants that look too small. Feel free to change the length of the legs to suit your personal preferences.

- Fold down. Make a crease where you want to see the hem. Press the fold so that it is flat and check it to see if you have folded it properly. Once you have done it on one side, measure it just under the original hem and use this measurement to create a similar fold on the other leg.

- Keep it in place. Put needles all around the leg of the pants to hold it in place. Make sure that the seams are aligned on the same leg and aligned with each other.

- Sew the hem. Sew stitches all around the leg of the pants just below the points of the original hem. You can do it with a sewing machine or by hand. Now you have to sew the back of your leg before folding it in later. This will allow you to pull out the hem later if you are growing up or want the pants to be longer.

- Unfold the hem. Push the excess fabric into the leg of the trousers by folding the original hem down so that the outer side can be seen. This should leave a small loop of fabric along the edge of the jeans inside the leg. Try your jeans to make sure it's the right length.

- If you do not think that you will ever want to have longer pants, you can also cut the end of the fabric. Cut the excess fabric about 2 cm from the hem you just made.

- Iron the jeans. Use an iron to flatten the hem that you have created along the edge. This will flatten the fabric loop inside while getting pants to the right length without any sign of changes.

Create a new hem

- Make a mark at the location of the hem. The best way to do this is to put on your pants (or ask someone to wear it) and bend your lower leg until you get the length you like. Then use a piece of chalk to mark where you want to see the hem.

- Measure and mark two more lines. Measure 1 cm from the hemline and draw a line above parallel to the first. Then measure another 1 cm and make a mark below the original line and draw a new line parallel to the first.

- You should now have three lines. They will serve as a guide to sew the hem.

- Cut along the bottom line. Cut the bottom of the pants and the old hem. To do this, simply cut a straight line along the bottom line that you have drawn. Discard the fabric you just cut.

- Fold the new hem from below. Then, fold it along the middle line to make the new hem. You should also put needles to hold it in place while you sew it. Make sure the hem is in place all the way around before you start sewing.

- Sew the hem you just folded. Take gold

thread for your choice of jeans or yarn and sew all around the area you have just held with the needles. Use a straight stitch and try to keep it as even as possible.

- Take out the needles as you go.

- After sewing the two hems, your jeans are ready to wear!

How to make DIY Ripped jeans

- Buying already torn jeans can be expensive. But, good news! It's easy to tear up yours. By following the right steps, with the right material and patience, you can quickly and easily rip your jeans.

- Choose jeans that fit you well. You can rip any jeans and get the same result, but do not feel obliged to rip one that you already have since you can find other cheap ones in thrift stores.

- Using jeans that have already been worn a bit will give better results than brand new jeans, but do not stop if you want to buy a new one for this project.

- Washed light-colored jeans are usually prettier when torn, as their color gives them a more worn look. The darker faded jeans seem too freshly dyed to be torn and will not be as "realistic".

- Gather your materials. All you need to tear your jeans are jeans and a sharp object. However, depending on the style you want, you will probably need to use a cutting tool.

- If you want to make holes, use scissors, a razor, or a sharp knife. The cutters also work.

- To create a frayed look, use sandpaper, cheese grater, or pumice.

- Choose a place to tear. Spread your jeans on a table and use a pencil to mark the places you want to rip. Use a ruler to mark the exact length you want. Keep in mind the last cut as well as the length, and the width of the holes.

- Generally, most people only tear at the knees, although it is possible to tear the lower legs of the jeans.

- Just aim a little higher than your knee so that the tear does not become too big when you walk. Whenever your knee bends, it will take in the hole and tear it further.

- Do not tear too high.

- Spread the jeans on a flat surface. Slip a small piece of wood into the jeans' legs as you relax, so that you do not change the front and back of the jeans.

If not, you can even use cardboard, an old book, a stack of magazines, or anything else you can cut without worry. Do not do it on the kitchen table if you use a very sharp knife.

- Start fraying the jeans with the sandpaper. Before you start cutting, use sandpaper or iron straw to start scrubbing and thinning the place you want to tear. This will help you soften the fibers of the jeans and make it easier to tear.

- Use a lot of different tools; alternate between sandpaper, iron straw, and pumice stone. It may take a little while depending on the thickness of your jeans.

- If you prefer to just cut jeans, go for it. You do not have to weaken it unless you want it to look frayed.

- Soften the fibers further to make holes. If

you want frayed areas and threadlike bands, use your scissors or knife to pull the area you have weakened with sandpaper. This will soften the fibers, letting a little skin appear when you wear jeans. Pull the white threads that come out of the jeans to exaggerate the look.

- Add holes with the knife or scissors. Take your scissors and cut a small piece of the relaxed area. Cut a little bit. You can still enlarge it, but you risk ruining your jeans and make it difficult if the hole is too big. Aim for a tear no larger than one centimeter.

- Make the tear in the direction of the width, not from bottom to top. It will look more natural.

- Use your hands to tear the jeans further. The tearing will pull on the fibers and give them the appearance of a real hole.

Pull the strings out, as if they were real tears.

- Avoid cutting the hole too much, as this will give it very clean and unnatural edges.

- Otherwise, you can just make a small hole and let it grow as you wear your jeans. It will look more natural that way.

- Reinforce your jeans if you want. To prevent the holes from getting larger, reinforce them by sewing around their perimeter. Use white or blue thread to sew around the tear, by hand, or machine.

- Go out with your cool jeans!

Advice
- Washing the jeans right after tearing them will make the fibers soften more and give an even more faded look.

- Avoid adding tears near the seams as they may start to distort.

- For an even more worn look, you can add bleach stains.

- For precise tears, use a sewing needle to pull the stitches one by one.

- If you are a man, avoid tearing too high, otherwise, we will see your underwear. For women, do the same by not exposing too much skin near your underwear.

Adding Frills to Your Jeans

You can use different styles of fabric to patch your jeans or to just add more decoration to them. One easy way to do this is to incorporate doilies and store-bought frills into your jeans. Using doilies to patch your jeans will create a really interesting pattern in the holes. You'll still see some skin through the hole, but you'll also have a lovely bohemian look to your jeans.

The Technique

To add doilies to your jeans, you'll need some thread that matches your jeans color, and a doily that looks nice and has already been washed. If you need to cut your doily, make sure that you hem the cut ends, so it doesn't unravel.

- Place the doily behind the hole in your jeans. Pin it to the jeans carefully to ensure you're not closing the jeans.

- Once everything is pinned, use a basic running-stitch to stitch the doily around the hole in your jeans, about 1.5 cm out from the hole itself.

- Do a second row at 1 cm away from the hole, to make sure that the doily is secure and won't move after being washed.

- Tie off the thread and cut it, hiding the ends inside the jeans.

To add doilies to the outside of your jeans, like on the sides or at the pockets, you can use washable fabric glue to add the doily to the fabric. You can follow these same techniques for adding frills, lace, or crochet to your jeans.

How to make DIY Frayed jeans

While some have found their happiness in the shop, others have instead chosen the economic option of DIY by manufacturing their frayed hem on old jeans. It's a technique that's easy to master, provided you do it right. Here's a very simple little tutorial on how to make a frayed hem without screwing up your jeans.

- Take your tape measure and start by accurately measuring the length at which you want to place the hem.

- Pin where you want the hem to finish and fraying to start.

- Whatever you do, do not forget that the operation will shorten the length of the jeans a little and multiple machine washes will add to it.

- Once you are done pinning, use your

scissors to cut the fabric as straight as possible.

- Then use your tweezers to pull some threads and fray your jeans.

- To complete the whole, perfect the operation, take some sandpaper and extract some more thread from the jeans.

- That's it, it's over, and you can put on your jeans! Obviously, the technique is also valid for any other piece of the same style such as a dress, shorts or denim skirt.

Why should you NOT wash your jeans?

The mistake that most people make is to think of jeans as regular pants. Jeans are not like a cotton chino that you can machine wash as often as you want. Would you wash your suit pants in a machine? Well, jeans have their specificities that must be respected, especially when they are raw jeans of good quality. Incidentally, if you have ecological beliefs, know that if the clothing lovers only wear raw jeans, it's because the canvas was not treated with chemicals like faded jeans. If your jeans are ripped, torn or worn out too much, washing them before mending them will only cause the damage to get worse. It is best to first fix the damage in your jeans and then wash it, if you must.

However, whatever the quality of your jeans, you must avoid washing it too often. And if you value your quality jeans, you should try hand washing them rather than a washing machine cycle.

How to mend and style thrift store finds

Buying from thrift stores efficiently takes time, but you can find beautiful, functional items for your home and wardrobe without breaking the bank. In addition, when you shop at charity bargain stores, you can support worthy organizations that help your less fortunate neighbors.

To develop a good second-hand store strategy, understand the differences between the different types of stores that sell used goods. For example, you will not find many high-end brands in standard thrift stores, but mail-order stores often sell branded clothing in good condition. What you can do is fix and style the old clothes you find in a thrift store to give them a new life and a different look.

You can stitch small tears and add different fabrics to worn-out clothes. If you find an item that you really like, but needs some modifications or damage repair, consider repairing or resizing the item to suit you. You save so much money by buying second-hand clothes that you can still pay for small repairs.

The rapidly growing second-hand fashion market remains an economic, ecological and eco-responsible solution for extending the life of a garment. This craze is explained by an awareness of the wastage of clothing. To stock up, there are of course the charity shops you can find amazing things for a very cheap price. Consider:

- Adding sequins or lace to your finds
- Shorten long skirts or dresses and throw on a belt to freshen them up
- Switch the old buttons on cardigans or jackets with new buttons
- Replace the zipper on pants with new zippers

Tips!
- Make sure the piece is still in good condition

If it is really damaged, you can always ask for an

additional discount and repair it yourself at home. However, from experience, if the piece is too damaged or old, it is not worth it.

- Evaluate price and quality

What I mean is that you do not get too excited about the price. Even if it's really cheap, it's not necessarily worth it and the opposite is true! It's not because it's a bit more expensive than it's worth. We must evaluate the piece, its quality, the number of times you wear it, etc. too.

It is a mandatory step to not be fooled by the low prices of thrift stores. The garment can be damaged, the fabric too old and fragile, and so on. So feel free to touch the material, read the composition labels by focusing on the noble materials (cotton, silk...), and make an inventory of the garment in its entirety to ensure that there is no stain or no hitch.

I also advise you to check the tags which can be a good indicator with regards to the quality and durability of the garment. Keep in mind that the clothing has already lived and has been worn, so a piece of a low-end brand is not necessarily a good deal. In case of an unknown brand or lack of brand label, look at the seams and finishes. But of course, the decision is up to you!

- Go early to get the best stuff

This may seem obvious, but to put all our chances on our side, it is better to go early. You should know that most thrift shops add to their stores every day, so the best deals of the day go first. In the end, it's a bit like during sales. So, we get up early (and in a good mood) to maximize its chances of finding the rare pearl.

Thrifty requires a lot of patience. When entering a thrift store, keep in mind that it is not Zara, Mango, or any other brand of ready-to-wear, and that the brands, when there are there, are not always organized. You have no choice but to search again and again. Nevertheless, imagine the satisfaction of finding a beautiful piece that was there, buried in a tray among so many other vintage clothes and that no one has seen.

- Be open-minded to change

I know, sometimes we would like to find THE perfect outfit that makes us dream for weeks, to no avail. This can be discouraging, but it is necessary to persevere and not be blinded by this coveted garment. Because by having a precise idea of the desired piece, you end up being disappointed and no longer see the other pieces that have as much potential, if not more.

- Consider every aspect

There are two questions to ask yourself when you are about to make a purchase in a thrift store, which I think is essential: "Can I imagine this piece in a current outfit?" And "Do I really like this piece?". Admittedly, we do not necessarily go into a second-hand shop to add a vintage touch to a current outfit: some also go because it's a good way to create a very unique, personal style. Nevertheless, I observe that most people (me included) make mixes between modern and retro. But to be able to mix a vintage piece and not regret its purchase, we must be able to transpose it to our time and especially, do not force yourself to like a piece under the pretext that "it's vintage and cheap".

Chapter 5: 10 Sewing Tips!

Below are some tips about sewing both by hand and sewing machine to give you a little bit more information and insight into the sewing world. By remembering and practicing these tips, you will be able to approach any sewing project with confidence. Eventually, you will learn things from your own projects and will have your own tips to share with people.

If you are worried about not doing things the correct way, good news! There are plenty of little tips for sewing right.

Tip 1: Do not look at the needle
Do not fix your eyes on your needle. Take a wider look and see what's around the needle instead. Focus on the fabric and observe how it stands and behaves throughout the seam.

Tip 2: Define your creative project
Always remember to take the time to choose

your project carefully. It can be a response to a need, or just a small pleasure to create. In any case, take note of the material you will need and select your fabric according to your project (the yardage is very often indicated). Try to have a clear idea of what you want to accomplish before you start. This way, you will make sure to ace all of your projects by practice.

Tip 3: Work on things you know you will like

If necessary, download or buy a pattern that you cut or copy. The internet is full of free and paid examples, so take the time to choose your favorites! The more you like your project, the better you will be able to focus on it.

Tip 4: Take your time

When you start, you must avoid rushing too much. Take the time to sew your stitches one by one, readjusting if necessary. You will find it to be easier for you to sew right than if you sew at a higher speed like the professionals. You will adjust your speed eventually. For now, take it slow.

Tip 5: Draw a line with chalk

You can also draw your chalk line in advance.

Thus, at the time of sewing, you will only have to follow the line and be able to sew right without too much difficulty.

Tip 6: Train yourself

Before actually sewing your project, familiarize yourself with your sewing machine by sewing straight and parallel lines on a piece of fabric, such as a piece of cloth or clothing. Test different stitches and vary the tension and the length of the stitches to better understand your machine.

If you are sewing by hand, practice doing regular stitches that will inevitably be more aesthetic on a piece of trial fabric before you move onto the costly fabrics.

Tip 7: Prepare your fabric

Whether for clothing or accessories, you will need to wash and prepare your fabric! That means you will also need to iron it so that it is wrinkle-free and ready to work on. Preparing the fabric will also keep the bad surprises away. You will know how the fabric washes, if it shrinks, or loses color before sewing and putting effort on it.

Tip 8: Using a magnetic stitching guide

There are magnetic sewing guides to block your fabric. You can use these instead of pinning the fabric down or using wood hoops. Find these magnetic guides online or at your local craft store to give them a try. You never know which one of these techniques you will like better.

Tip 9: Move your needle

If you are learning to use the sewing machine, move your needle to the left if you want a seam allowance of 1cm. Move it until the distance between the right edge of the crowbar and your needle is 1 cm and then place the edge of your fabric along the right edge of the crowbar. Thus, you will sew a seam margin of 1cm.

Tip 10: Get started!

You have fallen for a fabric, you have your project in mind, and all your equipment ready. Now is the time to start! Do not postpone your projects. If you don't start when you are super excited about it, you will probably keep postponing it. With the help of this book and the internet, you can learn and master any stitching technique.

Conclusion

For millennia, knowing how to sew has been considered a plus in many societies. Thus, more and more people are talking about sewing, and not just clothing. Moreover, we notice today that a large number of people want to learn how to sew. If you are wondering why sewing is becoming a common hobby again these days, we have some answers below.

Because sewing is an activity that brings people together

To strengthen family ties or strengthen bonds with friends, sewing is a fun activity everyone can do together. Imagine having a friend who knows how to sew like you. When you talk, you can talk about your latest creations. She is impressed by what you have done, and you are impressed by what she did. Everyone asks the other to tell them how to do certain things. This will result in hours of passionate discussion where you will be able to join the conversation.

Children can both learn a crucial life skill while having fun with you when you are teaching them how to sew. Sewing can also be a way to get closer to yourself; to discover you in another aspect.

Because learning how to sew is easy

Learning sewing today is easy. All you need is a needle, some thread, maybe a sewing machine for beginners and some tools, and you're ready. There are a lot of courses, tutorials, tips, and free patterns on the internet that can be used to learn quickly and easily. Thus, with the prospect of learning easily, sewing becomes much more attractive and conceivable. But you have to know how to be patient and willing to practice before managing to sew the gown of your dreams.

Because knowing how to sew saves money

Learning to sew saves money. If for example a shirt loses a button, it can be replaced quickly, without spending too much money on a new outfit or a seamstress or tailor. You can also patch a garment quickly and wear it. But knowing how to sew does not only make it possible to patch, but also to sew brand new things from simple fabrics.

You can make invisibs, wallets, tea towels, bags, and even dresses for yourself. It will take time, but with practice, the speed comes, and we spend less money sewing than for a purchase in a store or shop.

Because you deserve to wear clothes that fit you perfectly

When you get comfortable in your sewing, you can create amazing things that fit you like a glove. No need to spend a ton of money on designer clothing due to their tailored fit.

If you see a high fashionable garment that you like, but you cannot afford to buy, you can choose your own fabric and sew the model of your choice. You can also create custom clothing that looks and reflects your personality. To wear tailor-made clothing and stand out without spending a fortune, learn sewing even if it's online. It's the best option, not to say it's the only one, for keeping up your wardrobe.

References

9 Sewing Skills You Gotta Nail to Become a Total Master. (2019, July 11).

Retrieved from https://www.mybluprint.com/article/wanna-be-a-sewing-master-first-you-gotta-nail-these-9-skills

DH News Service. (2013, April 13). Rafoogari: Art of darning. Retrieved from https://www.deccanherald.com/content/325696/rafoogari-art-darning.html

Racklin, M. (2019, March 25). Instead of hiding rips and tears, the visible mending movement turns them into art.

Retrieved from https://www.vox.com/the-goods/2019/3/25/18274743/visible-mending-sashiko-mending-fast-fashion-movement

Repairing Jeans with Invisible Mending.

(2018, April 10). Retrieved from https://closetcasepatterns.com/repairing-jeans-with-invisible-mending/

Sashiko Mending Is a Clothing Life Saver. (n.d.). Retrieved from https://www.diynetwork.com/made-and-remade/fix-it/repair-holes-in-pants-with-sashiko

WeAllSew. (2018, July 30). Basic Sewing Techniques for Beginners. Retrieved from https://weallsew.com/basic-sewing-techniques-for-beginners/

What is Rafoogari? (n.d.). Retrieved from https://craftatlas.co/crafts/rafoogari

Made in the USA
Coppell, TX
03 September 2021